# HOWARD BAKER'S
# WASHINGTON

W·W·NORTON & COMPANY·NEW YORK·LONDON

# HOWARD BAKER'S
# WASHINGTON

*An intimate portrait of the nation's capital city*

FIRST EDITION

Library of Congress Cataloging in Publication Data
Baker, Howard H. (Howard Henry), 1925–
   Howard Baker's Washington
   1. Washington (D.C.)—Description—Views.
I. Title.
F195.B14   1982      975.3'04'0222      82–6336
                                        AACR2
ISBN 0-393-01562-9

W. W. Norton & Company, Inc. 500 Fifth Avenue, New York, N.Y. 10110
W. W. Norton & Company, Ltd. 37 Great Russell Street, London WC1B 3NU

1 2 3 4 5 6 7 8 9 0

# ACKNOWLEDGMENTS

This book, an expression of personal experience, is also the fruit of collaboration and cooperation. I want in particular to thank my friend Don Kellermann for his persistent dedication in helping me organize the material and seeing it through to completion. Allan Porter, director of the Senate Photographic Studio, has been both accommodating and stalwart in assisting me in my photographic forays around the city. He has given his free time and expended his energy with an enthusiasm for the project that matched my own. To Joe Bailey, one of *National Geographic*'s most talented photographers, I owe a debt of gratitude for his wise counsel and critical eye. Capitol Police Under-Sergeant Rodney C. Eads facilitated the task of filming within the Capitol building. I'm deeply grateful for their time and efforts. Katy Barksdale's arduous service in hunting through my negative and print files as well as Karen Pritchard's research and Nancy Westheimer's editorial and design suggestions are much appreciated.

When we were boys growing up in Tennessee and I used to work for Howard Baker's family, I'd be out there on Saturday afternoon washing the car or cutting the lawn and I used to think about what would happen to us when we grew up. I always knew I'd end up with a tuxedo on going to dinners like this...but I never thought *he'd* be there.

Lonnie Strunk
A Toast to the Majority Leader
January 5, 1981

Inauguration of Ronald Reagan as president of the United States, January 20, 1981. Photograph by Basil Jewell.

The east front of the Capitol. Opposite: Capitol interiors. Above left: Senate Reception Room. Above right: Old Supreme Court Chamber. Lower left: Statuary Hall. Lower right: Detail, Statuary Hall.

15

The real warmth and closeness I feel for the Capitol and its places didn't come to full flower until after I'd been there a long time. I had shown countless constituents around the Rotunda and the Senate wing and, occasionally, the House of Representatives. I began to pick up by osmosis, more often than not by an accidentally overheard lecture by Capitol guides, some of the historical significance of the Capitol. I began to *feel* the history in which its stones are soaked.

Senator Norris Cotten of New Hampshire got it right. On one of the first days I was in the Senate, he said, "Howard, can you smell the white marble?" And I said, "Norris, white marble doesn't have any smell. Marble doesn't smell." He said, "Oh, yes it does. And when you smell it, you'll be ruined for life."

I began to smell that marble, and then I began to realize that the Capitol is sort of like the country. It is a hodge-podge. It had modest beginnings, and it was nobly but perhaps poorly conceived. I refer to the false starts—the bungling and bickering of the Revolutionary and post-Revolutionary periods. It was the magnificence of the Constitution that redeemed the dream in 1789 and gave lasting structure to our politics. So it was with our poorly conceived Capitol. George Washington hired Dr. Thornton—a physician, not an architect by training—to design the Capitol. He was probably a pretty good doctor, but, sadly, he was not much of an architect. It was Benjamin Latrobe who finally rearranged and redesigned and largely rebuilt the Capitol. He was, in a sense, the man who built a stone edifice to match the new Constitution.

It was modest in its concept, faltering in its beginnings, with two fairly small chambers connected by a wood corridor. It had very little ornamentation. In 1814, the British burned it. That turned out to be a blessing, because it gave Latrobe and others the opportunity to rebuild the Capitol with structural integrity.

The Capitol is first of all a workplace. The awe a new member feels at his surroundings disappears very quickly. An old Senate story goes to the heart of it. It's about the freshman senator who wonders for a year how he got here, and the second year he wonders how all those old goats got here before him. So, it is above all a place to work, and I think of it in just the same way I used to think of a courtroom or my law office.

Mike Mansfield's experience is very much to the point. When he retired as Senate Majority Leader in 1977, he had completed thirty-four years of service in Congress, during which he moved around the Capitol from committee room to committee room, from caucuses to hearings, at the very center of the work of the Congress. Before moving on to take up his post as ambassador to Japan, Senator Mansfield and his wife took a tour of the Capitol so that they could "see" for the first time the monuments, the statuary, the symbolism of the place in which he had excercised great influence for most of his adult life.

The building has continued to expand and grow with nooks and crannies and contrivances to house the two chambers and the Library of Congress and the Supreme Court and, initially, the president. At one time the entire government of the United States worked in the Capitol. Then, in the 1850s, at the very height of the controversy over the survival of the Union and great issues like slavery, two new wings were added. One hundred thirty years later, we still speak of the Senate Chamber as the "New Chamber," as distinguished from the original. After the Civil War we built this new Capitol, and we have continued to enlarge it.

There is, today, a continuing and ravenous debate about adding to the west front. The wall is deteriorating, and we're going to replace it, or it's going to crumble and fall. The question now occurs: Are we

17

Interior of the Capitol dome from the rotunda.

Opposite: Washington chandelier, Little Rotunda, Senate wing of the Capitol.

going to replace it as it is, or are we going to extend it 106 feet, and add all sorts of new expense. Or, are we going to burrow out under Jenkins Hill and build a great underground parking mall. I rather suspect that the Capitol is going to continue to grow, just like the country.

But I hope we never lose the flavor of the past. To this day we are reminded of that past when pictures are taken inside of the Majority Leader's office. You level the camera with spirit levels and take the picture, and those walls aren't straight. That worried me because I thought my camera was out of plumb, but it wasn't. When I put the level on the wall, I found that it was the wall itself that was out of plumb. But those walls, plumb or not, have stood through two hundred years in which a good deal of work and some mischief, too, has been done, and working within them, I never cease to feel connected to the history of this country.

I have a particularly strong affection for the part of the Capitol that I am fortunate to occupy. My wife's father, Senator Dirksen, occupied it, and so did other heroes of mine, such as Bob Taft and other Republican leaders back through time. But the personal associations account for only part of its fascination.

The Majority Leader's Office is the oldest occupied space in the Capitol. It's the space in which the House of Representatives met when the government first moved to Washington in 1804. Sometimes I think about that, and I tell visitors that these are the rooms occupied by the first House. It puts in perspective how young and how small the country was, because then there was one entire body of Congress comfortably seated in a fairly small group of rooms. It's in this space that Thomas Jefferson defeated Aaron Burr for the presidency on the thirty-fourth ballot. There had been no majority in the electoral college, and the House of Representatives decided the presidential election in that year.

Later these same rooms were the first Library of Congress. There were just over three thousand volumes in the Library then, and it was to this place that the British came in August of 1814 when they set fire to the building. They took the books off the shelves and burned them.

The fireplace in my private office was something of a pleasant surprise to me. During the years Ev Dirksen was Minority Leader, I heard him complain on several occasions that since they air-conditioned the Capitol, it had been necessary to seal the fireplaces. Like most everything else Dirksen said, I accepted that at face value. But when I first came to this space as Leader, I was standing by as the furniture was being arranged and my personal paraphernalia was being moved. I asked a maintenance man, more musing to myself than anything else, what it would take to put that fireplace into service. He said, "Well, some kindling and a match, I suppose."

I discovered recently that the exact duplicate of this fireplace mantel resides in the White House. I read an *Architectural Digest* story about how Dolley Madison had summoned Benjamin Latrobe, who was then working on the Capitol, to come and help tidy up the new White House. That was when I first realized that when Latrobe went down to help Dolley Madison, he took one of my mantels with him. I don't think I have the courage to tell Nancy Reagan that I want my mantel back, even though it's one half of an exact and matched pair.

Hanging opposite the mantel is one of the few important paintings done from a photograph. When Abraham Lincoln and his ten-year-old son Willie went to Mathew Brady's studio in Washington to have their picture taken, someone saw them in a thoughtful and poignant pose and caught the moment. Willie Lincoln died in 1862. He was twelve years old.

The old mahogany table in the Majority Leader's office is refinished once a year. We do that because at the end of each session its surface is

Majority Leader's desk and sitting area.

Opposite: Conference table in the Majority Leader's suite.

Senate and presidential staff at work in the Majority Leader's office. Below: Senate Secretary William Hildenbrand tallies votes for a bill before the Senate. Opposite: President Reagan in the Majority Leader's office.

completely pitted. It may be that people banged down water glasses, or scratched it with their fingernails, or dropped their cigars, or whatever. Significant decisions have been made around that conference table. The Civil Rights Act of 1964 and the Fair Housing Act were hammered out there, and much of the strategy for the passage of the AWACS sale to Saudi Arabia was decided there, too. On the Panama Canal Treaty the great conflicts really never occurred on the floor. We came on over here from the Foreign Relations committee room to wrestle it down. The determination to have a bipartisan approach to great issues has been made here and so have decisions to fight. This table would be in an acute state of distress if we didn't pay close attention to its physiological needs. We do, because in many ways it is one of the private centers of Congress, as the dome is its public center. I remarked once to President Reagan that I thought this room offered the best view in Washington. He promptly and directly told me that it might be the second best view, but he had the best one.

---

AS PRESIDENTIAL HOMES GO, THE WHITE HOUSE is very nice, but it is by no means what you would expect as the residence of an "imperial president." It isn't nearly as big and striking as the palace of the governor of Puerto Rico. It doesn't compare, really, with the presidential palaces in Colombia or Peru, and it can't hold a candle, of course, to most of the presidential and regal houses in Europe. I think that is proper and adds to its dignity.

In some ways, you come to realize that the White House, like the Capitol, is what the Republic is all about. The founding fathers had simplicity and even severity in mind when it was conceived. But, I have often wondered if they ever intended that the presidential business would be transacted there. The East Wing and the West Wing,

Secret Service agent prepares for a presidential appearance.

Marine guard outside the Oval Office.

Opposite: The White House from Lafayette Park.

added later for executive office space, are appendages that add nothing architecturally to the building. And I do think that, as are some of the other public buildings in Washington, the White House is misplaced. They must have gotten a good deal on the price of that piece of land! In one direction it faces the Hay Adams Hotel across Lafayette Park and then it goes to nothing. It's as if somebody decorated a splinter on a spoke.

Regardless of the suitability of its location, the White House is probably the last and best embodiment of federal and early American decoration. But it isn't especially functional. It is not large enough to accommodate many of the groups that should be involved in White House affairs, and the decorations really do tend to venerate the past rather than to identify with the present or the future. It's a building that is destined for change. What ought to happen is that the working part of the White House should be moved somewhere else. I would like to see it return to the Capitol, where it was first located and where I have always believed it belongs.

While I'm at it, I might as well reveal that I have also always resented a little the placement of the Treasury Building in its position of next-door neighbor to the White House. It blocks the view, the line of communication between the Capitol and the White House. And *that* was a perfect example of an overweening use of presidential power. Old Andrew Jackson, when he entered the White House, asked a group of commissioners to select a site for the new Treasury Building. When they took their time about coming up with a location, Mr. Jackson stalked out of the White House, stomped his cane on the ground and said, "Build it here." He walked back to the White House, and that is where it was built. In the 1980s that would probably have been cause for a constitutional confrontation.

Statue of General Andrew Jackson in Lafayette Park.

White House council Fred Fielding and Senators Strom Thurmond and Robert Dole exit White House meeting.

Congressman Barber Conable, Vice-President George Bush, and Congressman Delbert Latta at the White House.

Presidential assistant Lyn Nofziger and President Reagan.

Conference table, White House breakfast meeting.

Within the White House the Oval Office can be the most intimidating place. It's been invested with awe by history, tradition, and popular journalism. It is a handsome room, but it was obviously an afterthought. I have sometimes reflected that it is odd that the seat of power for this Republic is situated in a part of the building that is adjacent to the original structure, connected by a breezeway to it, and designed and constructed a century after the original White House. It's almost as if they didn't think of the presidency until much later. But until Teddy Roosevelt's time cabinet meetings were held on the third floor in what is now a sitting room. Treaties were signed there, and business was transacted in the living quarters.

Being intimidated or overawed by the room or the building, the occupant, or the history of the place is a big impediment to common sense and reason and judgment. Of course that's one of the weapons and one of the tools of the presidency. And presidents depend on it. Every one of them must, to a degree, use that weapon of intimidation in order to lead. There are interesting tensions at play, because if you're going to work with the president, you can't afford to feel like an extra in the chorus line.

Not long after President Reagan took office and the Republicans gained the majority in the Senate, I was stopped at the Northwest Gate of the White House and asked for identification. I showed it to an officer, who went back to call in the identification and to see if I was expected. He then came back and asked for my Social Security number. He then went back and called again and then, somewhat grudgingly, admitted me through the Northwest Gate in my chauffeur-driven Senate automobile. By then I was seething. I don't like to confess that my ego had been injured, but it had been. When I got into the Oval Office, I said, "Mr. President, I don't know when you're

Majority Leader's automobile.

coming to the Capitol next, but the next time you come to our turf, you make sure you've got lots of good identification."

I was stopped by the Secret Service once in Memphis when I was with a presidential motorcade, and I was diverted because I didn't have the right pin on. When I rejoined Gerry Ford, I couldn't help but feel that presidents are nice to have, but they're hell to be around. Presidents are a lot of trouble, because the office is so immersed in the trappings of power, the necessities of protection. I sometimes think that Secret Service people must be born with an inability to smile. All in all it's a very difficult life style for the president's principal staff—as well as for the man himself.

Senators John Tower, Mark Hatfield, and Assistant Secretary of State Powell Moore at the White House.

President Reagan sends his autograph to Congressman Jack Kemp's son.

Above left: Presidential counselor Edwin Meese and Budget Director David Stockman.

Middle: Secretary of the Treasury Donald Regan and Presidential Chief of Staff James Baker.

Lower left: Congressman Barber Conable, Vice-President George Bush, Senator Paul Laxalt, and Congressman Tom Evans.

Above: President Reagan and former Republican Leader John Rhodes.

Conference table in the Roosevelt Room, the White House.

Views of the Potomac. Above: Rosslyn, Virginia, skyline.

Opposite: Skaters in front of the Arlington Memorial Bridge.

The tidal basin in spring. Opposite, above: Mount Vernon. Below: The mall from the Capitol.

44

National Park Service tour of the C & O Canal, Great Falls, Maryland. Guides at the stern of the barge.

Opposite: Canal bank from the barge.

48

C & O Canal tour. Opposite: Barge
on the canal. Right and below:
Guides at Civil War campsite.

Newspaper vending machines at National Airport, August 8, 1981.

Senator John Tower and ABC News correspondent Sam Donaldson outside the White House.

Senators Claiborne Pell, Joseph Biden, John Glenn, Paul Sarbanes, Edward Zorinsky, Paul Tsongas, Alan Cranston.

Secretary of State Alexander Haig at his Senate confirmation hearing.

President and Mrs. Gerald Ford leave Washington, January 20, 1977.

President Jimmy Carter.

Henry Kissinger and former President Gerald Ford.
Opposite: President Jimmy Carter with former Presidents Gerald Ford and Richard Nixon after memorial services for Senator Hubert Humphrey.

Flags honor King Juan Carlos.

Opposite: King Juan Carlos.

Podium at state visit ceremony, White House lawn.

Nancy and Henry Kissinger.

The hostages coming home.

ONE OF THE JOYS OF PHOTOGRAPHY is that it may be the only place where I can reasonably aspire to perfection. I can *never* do that in politics, in Congress, or in personal relationships. Perfection is destructive and corrosive if you apply it to things other than those things that you can pick up and lay aside. But photography is two-dimensional. Color balance is absolute and impartial. Shape and form can be defined. And, though I may not achieve a work of art or even an attractive photograph, I can channel the desire to achieve perfection into this pursuit.

Politics is demanding, and the Senate is especially so. My schedule is always unpredictable, so with me photography is of necessity a hit-or-miss proposition. But I've been at it a long time. When I was young, I was frequently asked to take pictures of funerals. I did a big trade in taking pictures of cadavers. That opportunity came because in my part of the country bodies were usually laid out at home, in an open casket, the day before the funeral. Since I was known as a photography nut, I was often asked to come and take a picture of the newly departed dear one. I did a big trade and was usually paid some small amount of money for taking pictures of corpses. Having survived that apprenticeship in good spirit, I have reason to believe that taking pictures and bringing them to life is a commitment that won't change. For one thing photography is filled with surprise. There are always unexpected revelations.

One of the best examples was the first picture I ever took of Elizabeth Taylor. And this says nothing about my photography but a great deal about Elizabeth Taylor. She and John Warner asked me to take their picture outside the Capitol with the dome in the background. John planned to use it in a political publication with my by-line on it as a tiny additional political feature. It was a routine picture that was taken hundreds of times, thousands of times a year by countless photographers. Even before I saw the print, while the negative was still in the enlarger, her eyes came blazing out—like nothing I had ever seen. They were almost mesmerizing. And then when I printed it, those violet-blue eyes stood out as though they were iridescent. It's hard to describe the impact of that experience because Elizabeth is very different in person. She's highly attractive and a very warm person. But that photograph was almost mystical.

Those photographs that generally appeal to me are straightforward and simple and direct. I could say that they are almost quiet. That may be because my life is so hectic and full of controversy that the quietness of a photograph is a thing of beauty. I was once asked to judge a White House press photographers' contest. There were two other judges on the panel with me. I can recall considering one picture in particular. I was in sharp disagreement with my colleagues, who saw no particular merit in the photograph. It was the image of a kayak going over a white-water fall. It was stark and it was simple...a tiny point of humanity in a great sea of foam. It was black and white, and not really very good from a technical viewpoint. But it was a beautiful statement of a person alone in time of peril; and I could feel his uncertainty from that photograph. I suppose it did not have the dynamism and the energy that others had, but it said something important to me. I don't think it even placed in the contest.

The pope's hat.

The pope's Mass on the mall.

Senator Barry Goldwater.

Panda: The National Zoo.

Ford's Theatre

L

Senator John Stennis.

Opposite, left: Senator Robert Byrd. Right: Senator S. I. Hayakawa. Below: Senator Alan Cranston.

Right: Senator Strom Thurmond. Below left: Secretary of Defense Caspar Weinberger and Secretary of State Alexander Haig. Below right: Senator John Warner and Elizabeth Taylor.

Left: House Speaker Tip O'Neill and Joy Baker. Above: Elizabeth Taylor and young friend, Eileen Hoffman. Below: Art Buchwald and Dinah Shore. Opposite: Senator Robert Byrd.

Above: Garden party at the White House.

Opposite: First Lady Nancy Reagan and Joy Baker at the White House.

WASHINGTON IS VERY MUCH A PEOPLE'S CITY. It's a place where people come out into the streets and parks to enjoy the green and stately façades that stamp the words "public place" on almost every aspect of the city's life. Just now in its development, it is a town with a magnetic appeal for the younger generation. I was uncomfortable with the almost carnival atmosphere that developed in the 1960s and 1970s in Georgetown, not only because it made traffic almost impossible to endure or because of the pervasive aroma of marijuana invading the nostrils as you walked down the sidewalk. It just seemed that a historical city deserved better than that. But that's subsided and been absorbed now, and the residue has given the city a vibrancy that it didn't have before. Washington has absorbed the Vietnam generation with ease and some attractiveness. We have a great concentration of young men and women either just out of college or, in many cases, still in college—young professionals who want the experience on the Hill or at the Internal Revenue Service, the State Department, the Justice Department, and the like.

When I was a boy, I had a great aunt who was Congressman Kenneth McKellar's secretary. My impression in those days was that most of the folks who worked in Congress were old. Maybe that was because I thought of my great aunt as an old spinster lady, or maybe it was truly the case. But today Washington has a very youthful cast of characters on display, and these young people have brought a special quality with them. They contribute enormous vitality to the city. They're the joggers and the bicycle riders, the volleyball, football, and hockey players. They're the ones who make such a diversity of fun on a Sunday afternoon in the spring and summer when you see everything from a jousting tournament to a tennis match. They're the ones who carry their children on their backs papoose style and wade in the reflecting pool. They may be a rebellious generation, but they don't

Opposite: Onlookers at a jousting tournament.

Left and opposite: Outdoor
Washington.

act it; they act as though they have a respect and even an affection for
the national monuments and traditions.

I met a young couple near the Washington Monument who sum up,
very sweetly, many of the young people who make the city a part of
their lives en route to other places and times. They were married and
they jogged every day. They saw me taking pictures and came over and
said hello and very sadly added, "We are taking our last jog." He had
finished his graduate work in communications at American Univer-
sity and had just been offered a job with the television station in some
town in Texas. They found it hard to describe their feelings. They
were sad. They were going away, but they hoped to come back to
Washington some day. It was as though they had already begun to
flavor the memory of their last jog along the Potomac and past the
monuments.

Opposite and above: Competitive Washington.

Touring the capital city.

Outside the Folger Shakespeare Library.

Opposite and above: Washington street scenes.

Washington water scenes.

While Washington is a perfect place to bicycle and jog and photograph, it surprises us with its old houses—sometimes very large houses and estates—tucked away in the privacy of sheltered neighborhoods from Kalorama to Georgetown. At the same time it is a city that promises to be one of the world's foremost cultural centers. It is a remarkable thing to see tourists by the millions who visit their capital and line up for blocks to see the new East Wing of the National Gallery, the Corcoran Gallery, the Smithsonian Institution, or the many other cultural and historical buildings throughout the city.

The Smithsonian calls itself "the nation's attic." That's not truly a fitting description because it is much, much more than that. I believe it is the premiere organization in Washington and perhaps in the country. It is innovative enough to attract millions of people to its excellent exhibits, ranging from natural history to representations of the latest lunar landing and photographs from Mars. It is traditional enough to house and protect some of the world's great treasures.

I recently watched as the big pendulum in the American History Museum swung back and forth. The pendulum marks the rotation of the earth and all around on the floor there were youngsters from every part of the country who were laying down on their stomachs mesmerized by this thing. Those were little children, little kids four and five and six years old. And on another floor of the same building, you'll find an entirely different group of people. They might be the mothers and fathers of those children, and they are looking at the Hope Diamond. If you walk a little farther down Constitution Avenue, you will find their older brothers and sisters in the Air and Space Museum.

The John Bull locomotive sits in the center of the Smithsonian, and it looks for all the world as if it's never been moved. The steam locomotive, retired from active service in 1865, was first exhibited as a museum piece at the Philadelphia World's Fair of 1876. For over one hundred years, it has graced the Smithsonian. One day last year somebody scratched his head and wondered "if that engine can still run or not." The Smithsonian went about finding out. They took it out to the C&O Canal, put it on the track, pumped up its innards with compressed air, fired it up, and it ran down that track as though it had never missed a single day's service. I don't know of any other museum in the world that would be so adventurous in spirit. That is reflected throughout the Smithsonian. But I think the quintessential Smithsonian gift is the eye it has on the future.

Octagon House.

Octagon House interiors. Above left: The state room. Above right: The dining room. Below: The restored kitchen.

Kaloramo Road houses.  Above: French embassy residence.

Above and opposite: "The Castle" of the Smithsonian Institution.

The Rotunda of the National Museum of American History.

The *John Bull* locomotive in the National Museum of American History.

The J. Edgar Hoover Building, FBI Headquarters. Below: The East Wing of the National Gallery of Art.

Two very different buildings seem to me to offer genuine architectural statements about Washington's future. One of them, the J. Edgar Hoover Headquarters of the FBI, has been criticized broadly both for its namesake and its appearance. There is no question that its massive, squat façade looming along Pennsylvania Avenue is in stark contrast to the gracious lines of the Palladian structures farther along the avenue. But it does say something about today and tomorrow. The same is true for the imaginative beauty reflected in the spacious sweep of I. M. Pei's East Wing of the National Gallery. There is an elegance to the East Wing structure unmatched in any of the city's older buildings.

Washington can take pride in the kind of expression that links the past to the future and offers an insight into the direction of our country to the millions of people who come to the city to enlarge their experience and their vision. But marvelous expressions though they are of the politicians' and planners' ideas of the dignity and heroic quality of the State, I personally think we have been mistaken in trying to emulate the structure of the Capitol, with its Greek columns and classical proportions, in almost all of the public buildings along our great avenues. The exception is the Lincoln Memorial—maybe because it is distanced from those on the other side of the mall from the White House and the Capitol. Whatever the reason, it is not subject to any canons of criticism I can bring to bear.

I have no such trouble when it comes to the Supreme Court. There is a building that is ripe for tearing down. Its only reason for being, I sometimes think, is to block the view from the Capitol. It somehow seems sterile, and, most important, it really should be farther out on the mall. The Court has space problems even now, and I don't doubt that someday it will be moved to a more suitable location.

United States Supreme Court.

Opposite, above: Restoring downtown Washington.
Below: Tourist bus.

Opposite, above, and overleaf: Washington relaxes.

The Washington Monument.

as it is, it stands out by itself, and it is ill placed and inappropriate to the design of the city in its present configuration. This may be why most people do not express the same sense of reverence that's so apparent at the Lincoln Memorial. I think Jefferson deserves better of posterity. He ranks with any of our national heroes. He may even be in a class by himself.

The Lincoln Memorial has a mystical quality. It's almost like a temple. It may be the result of its placement. It may be the reflecting pool. But I suspect that it's that statue. It has the flavor of the ark of the covenant, and it is the embodiment of the ambition and the sacrifice and the conflict that has shaped a caring nation with a social conscience. That quality is enshrined in the Lincoln Memorial. The lighting of the Lincoln Memorial has something to do with its effect. But the heroic size and that sad countenance, that lanky frame, that ultimate determination which may be partially the product of a manic-depressive personality, express a unique mingling of calm and pain.

We venerate Lincoln universally. But that wasn't the case while he lived. Not even Republicans, not even Unionists, gave him his due. He was thought of not only as authoritarian, but dictatorial. He trampled on the rights guaranteed under the Constitution. He effectively imposed martial law on this country without ever saying so. He ran off all except a few Democrats, because most of them went "over the hill." They defected, and they were rebels until we "put down the rebellion." That was the wording of the resolutions that were almost always included in every statute or law that was passed by the Congress. Today we say, "the welfare of the Republic requiring it." They used to say, "until the rebellion is suppressed."

I believe it was not until many years later that this universal reverence for Lincoln arose. Martyrdom had something to do with that. But while he lived, he always kept his eye on a single purpose, that of the preservation of the Union—the freeing of the slaves and the establishment of a new order. I'm uneasy at even acknowledging the theory of manic depression, because Lincoln was too large for labels. He was too kind, too determined to show compassion and care after the war, to be so classified. I wish my fellow Tennesseean, Andrew Johnson, had been deprived of the presidency. It would have been a blessing for Johnson and for the country because there would have been an entirely different reconstruction of the South under Lincoln. That lost opportunity for reconciliation is also immanent in his memorial. Perhaps it's anguish, a frustrated wish to show compassion that comes through. There's an ethereal expression of the sadness of death, certainly a premature death.

Similar values are expressed at the Kennedy grave, which was aligned, in a choice of genius, directly with the Lincoln Memorial and the Capitol and, later, the RFK Stadium on the other side. No amateur architects like our friend Dr. Thornton figured that out. That memorial will permanently give the martyr's aura to JFK—but it will not match the Lincoln shrine, because we do not have that heroic representation that comes from that serene figure sitting in that chair, in that throne of justice, in that seat of judgment, in that reminder of our commitment to social justice.

For me the most moving of all Washington's public places is the National Cemetery at Arlington. I have given it a lot of thought. The first thing that struck me about the cemetery—and this was when I was a small child and visiting Washington for the first time—was the enormous number of dead people. A child looking at that cemetery sees such a vast expanse and array of tombstones that it is almost overwhelming to his senses. I judge that adults often have the same feeling.

There are not many places on earth where the remains of the dead

The Jefferson Memorial.

The Lincoln Memorial.

Early morning at the Lincoln Memorial.
Opposite: John F. Kennedy Center for
the Performing Arts.

129

The Tomb of the
Unknown Soldier.

have been laid out in such an orderly and respectful manner. Although I have never been particularly impressed with the Tomb of the Unknown Soldier, it is, of course, an appropriate symbol. But I am much more moved by the simple fact that for most of our national life we have offered affection as well as respect to those who have sacrificed for the American Republic. I find it significant that the Arch of the National Cemetery lies along the architectural axis that reflects our national experience.

Linked by the Memorial Bridge to the Lincoln Memorial, the reflecting pool, and the mall, the cemetery seems to prove that we have not excluded those who served the nation from the still-unfolding life of our history. Most people put cemeteries in the suburbs; but we intentionally embraced those who are buried in the heart of our city and made them a part of the scheme of the life of the capital. This feeling becomes intensely personal as you walk or drive along and see the geometry of these small and uniform headstones. When you stop, there's a little shadow of the stones surrounding you. You look at the markers and read the names. Those names tend to stay with you.

Arlington National Cemetery.

Arlington National Cemetery.

Opposite: "Grief," Rock Creek Cemetery.

Honor Guard and tourist at the Washington Monument.

Secretary of State Alexander Haig and General David Jones, chairman of the Joint Chiefs of Staff.

THE FLAG IS OUR UNIVERSAL SYMBOL, and it touches deep and varied emotions. I have been photographing the flag since my first childhood visit to Washington in the 1930s. King George VI and Queen Elizabeth were visiting, too. I was staying with Aunt Mattie, and the Roosevelts put up the king and queen. There were British and American flags on almost every lamppost in Washington, and I believe I snapped them all. I was young enough for the panoply, the pomp and circumstance, and the trappings of the dramatic visit to have impressed on me for the rest of my life the importance of its symbolism. The flag expresses for most of us the life of our country and its hopes for the future. It's paradoxical that this symbol of life is also a touchstone at the ceremonies of death.

The flags around the Washington Monument are among the most striking groupings in the city. I recall as though it were yesterday the day I learned that my father had died of a heart attack. I was in Washington trying a law suit. When I heard the news, I headed for National Airport to go home to Tennessee, and as I drove down Constitution Avenue, I saw all those flags around the Washington Monument being lowered to half mast in salute to my father, a member of the House of Representatives.

The flag is pervasive in the capital city. You find it everywhere, from the White House to the Court house, from the Capitol to the schoolhouse. I take pictures of flags because they flap and flow in the breeze, they are pretty, and for reasons I probably don't understand.

The members of the Continental Congress who commissioned our first flag said it best when they ordered a banner of "thirteen stripes, alternate red and white, with a union of thirteen stars of white on a blue field, representing a new constellation."

Flags at the Washington Monument.

This book was designed by Nancy West-heimer with layouts by Ben Gamit. The type is Bembo, composed by Zimmering and Zinn, Inc., New York City. The book was manufactured by The Kingsport Press, Kingsport, Tennessee.